A Practical Resource for Negotiating the World of Friendships and Relationships

This is a practical resource for use by teachers, support staff and therapists that contains session ideas for use with children to promote kindness, friendship and self-compassion. It includes detailed lesson plans with extensive guidance and photocopiable activity sheets to support individuals, groups or classes of children aged 7 and upwards.

This guidebook can be used to:

- Help children understand the value of kindness, both to themselves and to others
- Nurture the moral development of children
- Support children who may be struggling with self-worth and self-kindness

This guidebook is available to purchase as part of a two-component set, *Negotiating the World of Friendships and Relationships: A 'Cool to be Kind' Storybook and Practical Resource*. It can be used by teachers, support staff and therapists to teach and promote kindness.

Liz Bates is an independent education consultant. She supports both primary and secondary schools in all aspects of Emotional Health and Wellbeing, including whole school approaches, training staff and delivering talks to parents. Liz is a Protective Behaviours Trainer, a Wellbeing Award Advisor for Optimus and a Schools Engagement Trainer for The Anna Freud Centre.

T0372244

A Practical Resource for Negotiating the World of Friendships and Relationships

LIZ BATES
ILLUSTRATED BY NIGEL DODDS

Routledge
Taylor & Francis Group

LONDON AND NEW YORK

First published 2021
by Routledge
2 Park Square, Milton Park, Abingdon, Oxon OX14 4RN

and by Routledge
52 Vanderbilt Avenue, New York, NY 10017

Routledge is an imprint of the Taylor & Francis Group, an informa business

British Library Cataloguing-in-Publication Data
A catalogue record for this book is available from the British Library

Library of Congress Cataloging-in-Publication Data
Names: Bates, Liz, author.
Title: A practical resource for negotiating the world of friendships and
relationships / Liz Bates; illustrated by Nigel Dodds.
Description: Abingdon, Oxon; New York, NY: Routledge, 2021.
Identifiers: LCCN 2020034626 (print) | LCCN 2020034627 (ebook) |
ISBN 9780367680008 (pbk) | ISBN 9781003133766 (ebk)
Subjects: LCSH: Friendship in children—Juvenile literature. |
Kindness—Juvenile literature. | Interpersonal
relations in children—Juvenile literature.
Classification: LCC BF723.F68 B37 2021 (print) |
LCC BF723.F68 (ebook) | DDC 155.42/492—dc23
LC record available at https://lccn.loc.gov/2020034626
LC ebook record available at https://lccn.loc.gov/2020034627

ISBN: 978-0-367-68000-8 (pbk)
ISBN: 978-1-003-13376-6 (ebk)

Typeset in Zag
by Newgen Publishing UK

Printed in the UK by Severn, Gloucester on responsibly sourced paper

Table of contents

Introduction

Scientific studies have shown that kindness has a great number of physical and emotional benefits and that children require a healthy dose of good, positive feelings in order to flourish as healthy, happy, well-rounded individuals.

Giving and receiving kindness are equally important. Being kind to others feels good, as does someone being kind to you. Being kind to ourselves is sometimes missed out – the final section of this resource will consider that.

Nurturing the moral development of children has both positive individual outcomes and also positive outcomes for others, for the group, for their peers, for the classroom.

The activities and learning in this pack explore:

Values – our personally chosen guide to behaviour. What are the qualities we most want to express in our behaviour? What do we most want to 'be about'? What is 'good' and why? What do we do that brings that to life?

Morals and principles – what are the 'rules' that we have, written or unwritten? How do they help us?

Empathy – what actions are compassionate? Do we think about the feelings of others and how our actions might affect them? Can we put ourselves in the shoes of others? Can we imagine what it must be like to be someone else – their feelings and thoughts – to mentalise?

Right to feel safe – do we have this right? Why is it an important right to have? If we have this right, do we also have the responsibility to uphold the rights of others to feel safe? We can use words like comfortable, happy, secure as well as safe.

Respect – respecting ourselves and taking care of ourselves without harming others and so respecting the wellbeing of others. If we respect ourselves, are we more able to respect others?

Wellbeing – being kind to ourselves and to others is a key ingredient in our wellbeing.

Harm – how might our actions harm others? Why is that a choice for some people?

How do we decide what is the right thing to do?

Kindness can change our brains by simply experiencing it. We can think and talk about kindness but that is not enough. Experiencing kindness is the best way to learn about it.

Kindness can …

• increase positive behaviour and help to create warm, inclusive environments where children can feel safe, secure, noticed and listened to; where children can belong
• increase the likelihood of forming relationships; children are more likely to be accepted if they are well-liked – kindness is a pro-social skill
• change a viewpoint when helping others less fortunate
• produce endorphins activating parts of the brain that are associated with pleasure – this can lead to good feelings
• lead to a release of oxytocin – this can increase individual levels of happiness
• result in 'helper's high' increasing a sense of self-worth
• increase levels of serotonin which affects mood and other aspects of health

All of these can lead to better mental health.

And remember 'kindness can be catching'.

This resource can help children to understand the value of kindness, both to themselves and to others. And to understand that they have a choice to be kind.

There is no escaping the rise of unkindness in its most evident, explicit and toxic form. The internet has allowed anonymity to enable a 'no rules' onslaught of unkindness which is almost impossible to challenge. Protecting children from this is a Sisyphean task, so part of this resource is aimed at helping children to access support and to tell someone if they are experiencing unmanageable unkindness.

The driving idea however is to introduce children to the notion that kindness and unkindness are choices and to interrogate and question the choices we make.

The sessions/lessons and activities will incorporate:

The language of kindness.

The choice to be unkind – why might someone choose to be unkind when there is a choice to be kind? What is in it for me if I choose to be unkind?

The continuum of likes.

What might someone feel, what might someone think and what might someone do?

How do our feelings and thoughts affect what we do and what we say?

Do we have to believe what our thoughts tell us?

Does it matter what someone else thinks? Why? Why not?

If I need help…

Difference, Friendship and Language as superpowers.

There is another element of kindness which also plays a crucial part in the lives of some young people and that is self-kindness or self-compassion; a lack of it can lead to a drive to be perfect which, when not achieved, becomes a threatening and sometimes uncontrollable aspect of their lives. Comparing and measuring one's own life by the apparent 'achievements' of others and perceiving only failure if not successful, has to be talked about and explored. Only this way can we, as adults, help children and young people to have their own internal measure and recognition of self-worth. The final session of this resource will look at helping children to recognise if their own measures are unfair and unrealistic, which can lead them to be unkind to themselves. This session can be used as a stand-alone resource to support children who may be struggling with this specific challenge, or as part of the whole resource.

So meet Coco, Otto, Ollie and Ling as they negotiate the sometimes tricky world of friendships and relationships, observing the unkindness of some and using their 'superpower', kindness, to change the lives of others. Explore with them what it means to be unkind, why that choice is sometimes made and how usually there is another choice – to be kind. Support children to see that kindness can be a cool choice to make, discover other 'powers' – the power of friendship, the power of difference, the power of language – and finally help children to consider self-compassion and being kind to themselves.

Some of the activities may be challenging for some children.

All the activities can be done with large groups and whole classes.

Some activities will work well in small groups eg nurture groups with specific children.

Some activities can be adjusted to work with a single child. You know the children best so please use this resource in the way that suits you. The resource is written as a guide but also includes direct instructions to children that can be said verbatim. These instructions appear *in italics*.

There are 6 sessions described in this resource plus the additional **'Self-kindness' session**. It is up to you how these are delivered – 6 sessions may become 8 or 12 depending on how much time you have to deliver the content. Because of the amount of discussion and the importance placed on hearing what children feel and think, 6 is not set in stone. This learning can take place at home, in a classroom, in a nurture room, in a counselling session, wherever there is a child who may benefit. Please read the whole resource before using it. You will then know exactly where you are heading and can choose to move activities around if you wish.

Let's do what we can to help children to make kindness their first choice, indeed, their default. As Henry James said, "Three things in human life are important: the first is to be **kind**; the second is to be **kind**; and the third is to be **kind**".

Liz Bates

lizslamer@gmail.com

Session 1
Cool

What's the coolest thing?

This session is designed to encourage children to talk about the things they think are 'cool'.

It will be important in this session to emphasise that it is ok to think differently from each other. We do not have to like the things that others like – even things our best friend likes. This is covered in more detail in Session 5.

Read pages 1–2 in the book *Cool to be Kind*.

Activity – What's Cool?

Everyone think about the coolest thing. It could be a person, an activity, a job – anything.

- *Being a top gamer?*
- *Having a YouTube channel?*
- *Being in a dance crew?*
- *Scoring the winning goal in the FA Cup?*
- *A character in a book or in a film?*

Now everyone say what their coolest thing or person is …

Adults go first!

Discussion starters

- *How do you decide what is cool? Who is cool?*
- *Who are the coolest people you can think of? Why are they cool?*
- *What does it mean to be cool?*

Are they people who are …

- *… admired?*
- *… liked?*
- *… looked up to?*
- *… positive?*
- *… confident?*
- *… someone that other people want to be with, want to know, want to hang out with?*
- *… someone you want to be like when you grow up?*
- *… someone you dream about meeting?*

Why are they cool?

Can anyone be cool?

Create a display of people and things that are 'cool'.

Read pages 3–4 in the book *Cool to be Kind.*

Discussion starters

- *Might it be cool to have a superpower?*
- *How do superpowers help other people?*
- *Name some superheroes you know of.*
- *What are their powers?*
- *How do their powers help other people?*

Activity – Superpowers

You will need a copy of **Appendix 1 – 'Superpowers'** for each child.

Design a superhero and answer these questions either through writing or discussion.

- *What superpower does your superhero have?*
- *Why have you chosen that superpower?*
- *If you could choose a superpower to have, what would it be?*
- *Why?*

How would you help other people if you had that superpower?

Activity – Poster

In a group, create a 'How to be a superhero' poster. Ask each child to think of a 'superhero' statement.

For example:

- "Stand up for justice"
- "Share"
- "Use your superpower wisely"
- "Do the right thing"
- "Be patient"
- "Help other people"
- "Wear your cape"
- "Choose to be kind to others"
- "Be kind to yourself"

Session 2
Coco and Kez

Exploring the feelings of ourselves and others

This session explores feelings by encouraging the children to consider how Kez might have been feeling.

Read pages 5–6 in the book *Cool to be Kind* and briefly discuss what happened.

Activity – Feelings

You will need a copy of *Appendix 2 – 'Feelings'* for each child.

Children can work alone or in pairs to complete the worksheet.

Now ask the children to share their thoughts by giving as many answers as possible for the following questions – there is much to learn here as you will find a range of responses. This tells us that people can feel differently about the same situation; there is no right or wrong way to feel.

The children can use their completed sheets to inform their answers. Please note that we are considering how Kez **might** have felt. Not how he felt. This is an important distinction as it helps to reinforce that there is not a right or wrong answer.

Discussion starters

- *How **might** Kez have been feeling before the match?*
- *How **might** Kez have been feeling during the match?*
- *Why **might** no-one know what Kez is feeling?*
- *Do you think his team mates considered Kez's feelings?*
- *Why do you think you have different answers to each other?*

Important learning

- Other people don't know what we are feeling. Our feelings are hidden inside us.
- Other people only see our actions, what we do. They may not understand our actions.

Further questions

Why might it be important to tell people how we are feeling?

(There is much more on this in the book *Ruby, Rafa and Riz. Feel, Think and Do.*)

This can lead into discussions around others judging us on just our behaviour and possibly disclosure of safeguarding issues. Please ensure you are clear regarding your safeguarding responsibility.

Might Kez's feelings affect the way he played? Why?

Activity – Noticing Our Feelings

You will need a copy of **Appendix 3 – 'How Might it Feel?'** for each child.

Ask the children to think about the physical responses we get when we are anxious or nervous. What happens to our bodies?

These might include:

- Wobbly legs
- Feeling sick
- Feeling hot
- Wanting to go to the toilet
- Shaky limbs

… there are many, many others

(There is more on this, including the reasons for them in the book *Myg and Me.*)

Draw pictures on the figure outline of all the warning signs someone might have.

Some children might want to stand up to show and talk about their picture with all the signs drawn on.

Discussion starters

- *If Kez was feeling anxious or nervous might this have affected how he played? How?*
- *If he had shaky hands might he drop the ball?*
- *If he felt sick might he have lost concentration?*
- *How can we control our 'shaky hands'?*
- *How does a professional goalie keep calm?*

Here it is important to talk about the fact that everyone gets anxious or nervous about some things — you could give them an example of a time when you felt anxious or nervous. Sometimes it is helpful to find ways to overcome these feelings — you could then tell the children what you did.

A professional goalie will need to overcome their anxieties or nerves. They will need to control their wobbly legs and shaky hands.

What other occupations can they think of where people will have to overcome their nerves?

An acrobat, a singer, an actor, an astronaut, a surgeon, an electrician, a teacher, a firefighter …

All these people will have ways of self-calming and now we are going to learn some.

Activity – Self Calming

You will need a copy of *Appendix 4 – 'Calm'* for each child – one sheet can be divided for two children.

- Breathing
- Relaxing
- Visualising
- Sharing

Take the children through each of the calming activities – see next page.

They can then draw a picture in each space, cut into four and keep in their desk, tray, pocket, a box to look at and remind themselves if they need to.

BREATHING	RELAXING
Imagine you are holding a mug of lovely hot chocolate. Take 4 seconds to breathe in through your nose smelling the lovely chocolatey smell. Hold your breath for a count of 4. Then take 4 seconds to blow out through your mouth to cool down the hot chocolate. Wait for 4 seconds. Repeat.	Imagine you are made of ice. Make your arms and legs stiff. Make all of your body stiff. Hold it for 5 seconds. Imagine the sun has come out and is shining right on you. Slowly, slowly you begin to melt. Your arms, legs and whole body gradually melt until you are a pool of water on the floor.
VISUALISING	**SHARING**
If you are anxious about being a goalie, doing a test, performing a play, reading aloud, singing a solo … or anything else, sometimes it can help to picture yourself doing that thing and doing it really, really well. Seeing yourself being successful and achieving what you want to achieve. How does that feel?	If you find that you are worrying over and over again about something it can help if you tell a trusted adult about your worry. They may not be able to make everything better but they may be able to help and support you. A trusted adult is someone you feel really safe being with.

Discuss other things the children can do to help them to calm when they feel anxious. (There are lots of ideas in the book *Myg and Me*.)

Read page 7 in the book *Cool to be Kind*.

So now we know what the superpower is. It's KINDNESS.

Did anyone have kindness as their chosen superpower in Session 1?

Why is kindness a good superpower?

Discussion starters

How did Coco use her superpower?

The learning here is to bring out exactly how Coco was kind.

Coco praised Kez's bravery. What did Kez do that was brave?

- *Kez volunteered when he didn't have to. When no-one else did. Kez enabled the match to be played. The team got medals instead of being disqualified.*
- *Coco showed she was on Kez's side. She stuck up for him. She didn't have to do what others were doing. She didn't join in with their unkindness. Coco chose to be kind. She realised how important Kez's actions were. The coach helped by agreeing with Coco and congratulating Kez.*

So KINDNESS can be

- *Standing up for someone*
- *Praising someone's actions*
- *Being considerate of someone's feelings*
- *Doing or saying something different from what others are saying or doing*

What else can KINDNESS be?

Session 3
Otto and Indra

Helping other people

This session considers kindness as a choice and suggests that we all have the capacity to be both kind and unkind.

> Read pages 8–10 in the book *Cool to be Kind* and briefly discuss what happened.

Discussion starters

- *Why do you think Indra brings samosas round to Otto's house?*
- *Why do some people choose to do kind things for others?*
- *Why do you think people throw rubbish into Indra's garden?*
- *Why do some people choose to be unkind to others?*
- *What are the possible consequences for choosing to be unkind?*
- *What are the possible consequences for choosing to be kind?*
- *Are we all capable of being kind?*
- *Are we all capable of being unkind?*

The learning from these discussion points is to recognise that we all have the capability to be unkind – whether it is teasing our younger brother, leaving a friend out of a game, shouting at a friend, not helping at home. What else?

Activity – My Map of Me

It is not necessary for every child to have a copy of **Appendix 5 – 'My Map of Me'** but they need to be able to see it – so one enlarged version could be displayed for everyone to see.

- *We are all made up of different parts – some nice and some not so nice. Some we want others to know about and some we'd rather keep hidden. It's ok. Everyone is like that. No-one is perfect.*

- *When we are aware of all of our parts, we can work to increase the good bits and decrease the not so good bits.*

Ask the children to think about how they could do this. The more they notice things about themselves the easier it is to make choices about behaviour.

Look at **Appendix 5 – 'My Map of Me'** as an example of the statements we could make about ourselves.

Adults go first!

You will need a body outline – drawn on the IWB or on flipchart paper. Choose four or five 'best parts' and four or five 'not so good' parts. Use things you have evidence of – 'shouty' part, forgetful part, joke telling part – nothing too personal. Label your outline with your statements. Colour code if possible.

Each child will then need a body outline – you could make copies of **Appendix 3** or they can draw their own outline.

Look at the example statements on **Appendix 5**. It is important that children choose their own – no-one can tell someone else what their parts are.

Children can use *some* of the example statements, if they apply, but encourage them to think of their own. Three or four of each or more if they want to. Each statement can be written on or cut out and stuck on the outline. Their best parts can be colourful, in big letters; their not so good parts can be tiny, much easier to make even smaller so they stop existing.

Activity – Three Acts of Kindness

Children to come up with three acts of kindness. As ever, you go first.

These acts do not have to be grand gestures, they could be as simple as smiling at someone in class that they don't know. It may help to discuss what these acts could be.

- For school
- For a friend
- For a family member

Encourage the children to talk about what their acts of kindness are and why they have chosen them.

How did Otto use his superpower?

The learning here is that Otto did some tasks that were easy for him but may have been hard for Indra.

Kindness can often be rewarded in unexpected ways – for Otto is was with delicious food. Sometimes it may be rewarded with just a smile and a 'thank you'.

But superheroes don't use their powers to get rewards, they use them because it is the right thing to do.

So KINDNESS can be

- *Giving someone an unexpected gift*
- *Helping someone out*
- *Doing a kind deed for someone – especially a job that the other person finds difficult*

What else can KINDNESS be? (All the acts they have chosen in the last activity.)

Session 4
Ollie and Nina

Being a friend

This session further explores empathy and interrogates how and why we make the choices we do.

> **Read pages 11–12 in the book *Cool to be Kind* and briefly discuss what happened.**

Remind the children of the activity in Session 2 when they were asked to reflect on how Kez might have been feeling.

Now ask them to think about how Nina might have been feeling before arriving at school for her first day?

(Possible suggestions – nervous, excited, scared, sick, happy, embarrassed, unsure, shaky, frightened. There may be positive and negative feelings, so again reinforce how we can all feel differently about the same thing. We can also feel more than one feeling at a time.)

Activity – Thoughts

You will need a copy of *Appendix 6 – 'Thoughts'* for each child. Each child will need three colours to write with.

On the worksheet in the first colour:

- *What might Nina have been thinking as she arrived at school?*
- *Write three answers if possible.*

(Possible suggestions – 'I hope I make some friends, I hope they like me, I wonder if it will be like my old school, I hope they understand me, I hope I can do the work ...'.)

Share answers and explore the reasons why she may have been thinking these things.

Ask *has anyone here ever been new to a school or a club or to a group? Would they like to share what they thought?*

As the adult you could share an experience with them – your first day at school, at university, at work.

Why do we have these thoughts?

Help the children to explore where these thoughts come from.

They often come from our fears, our expectations, our previous experiences, our sense of belonging, our hopes, our expectation of support.

They are also quite natural and normal to have. It is our way of preparing for danger. The thoughts help our bodies to prepare in case there is danger.

(There is much more on 'fight, flight and freeze' in the book *Myg and Me*.)

On the worksheet in the second colour:

• *What might Nina have thought when she heard people laughing at the way she speaks?*
• *What might Nina have thought when her bag was missing?*
(Possible suggestions – 'I hate it here', 'why are they so mean?', 'I want to go home'.)

These things will probably have reinforced all Nina's negative thoughts.

Discussion starters

So why did some children **choose** to be unkind to Nina?

• *Why were some children unkind to Nina?*
• *What might their thoughts have been?*

Encourage the children to think of more than one reason.
For example: they didn't know her; they didn't like her; they couldn't understand her; someone else dared them to do it; they were cross about something else and took it out on Nina; they wanted to make her cry; they wanted to feel superior to Nina; they were showing off to their friends.

For each answer ask if that is a reason to be unkind or in each case could they have **chosen** to say or do something kind?

For each of the examples above, or the reasons the children come up with, ask for alternative, kind actions.

Such as:

- they didn't know her / go and ask her name
- they didn't like her / just leave her alone
- they couldn't understand her / help her to pronounce some English words
- someone else dared them / say 'no' to the dare
- they were cross / tell a trusted adult what they are cross about
- they wanted to make her cry / ask themselves 'why do I want to be unkind?' and walk away
- they wanted to feel superior / ask themselves 'why?' and walk away
- showing off / find another way to impress your friends, by showing how kind you can be
- *What were Ollie's choices?*
- *Why might Ollie have chosen to do what he did?*

On the worksheet in the third colour:

- *What might Nina have thought when Ollie sat down to talk to her?*
- *What might Nina have thought when Ollie introduced her to his friends?*

Why do you think some people use Snapchat and WhatsApp to send unkind messages?

For example: it's easy, it's funny, no-one knows who sent it, someone else might persuade you to do it.

Recap on alternatives from earlier in this session.

Activity – A 'Cool to be Kind' Message

You will need a copy of *Appendix 7 – 'Send a Cool to be Kind Message'* for each child – one sheet can be divided for two children.

- *Why might someone choose to send an unkind message rather than a kind message?*
- *Sometimes people might send unkind messages to make them feel better about themselves, to make them feel like a better person. But in actual fact, sending a kind message probably does a better job at making you feel better about yourself and feel like a better person.*
- *If you could send Nina a Snapchat message, what could you say that would be 'cool to be kind'?*
- *Write Nina a 'cool to be kind' message.*
- *How did Ollie use his superpower?*

So KINDNESS can be

- *Thinking about when someone else might be feeling anxious*
- *Knowing you have a choice in what you do*
- *Making the right choice*
- *Feeling good about yourself, just through being kind to someone else*

What else can KINDNESS be?

Session 5
Ling and Danny

This session revisits the idea that difference is something to be proud of, to be enjoyed and to be celebrated.

Read pages 13–16 in the book *Cool to be Kind* and briefly discuss what happened.

Discussion starter

• *Do we all like doing the same thing?*

Activity – Same or Different

We all have things that we like and things that we don't like.

In groups of five, ask the children to find five things that they all like – tv programme, music, food, football team, pizza topping … (if they are in groups of four then they find four things and so on).

Then find five things that everyone in the group dislikes.

Then see if they can find something that each of them likes but no-one else in the group likes, so a different thing for each of them – or something that each of them dislikes but no-one else does.

Discussion starters

• *Why are there some things we like and some things we don't like?*
• *We are all unique – which means we will feel and think differently to each other just like we all look differently to each other.*

Activity – The Continuum of Likes

You will need a copy of *Appendix 8 – 'Like / Not Like Continuum Cards'* cut into two separate pieces

LIKE
NOT LIKE

Place each card on the floor with a distance between them to create a continuum. This is best done in a larger, uncluttered space – a school hall, a playground, a garden, a corridor, depending on how many children are taking part.

Read out each item from the list below and ask the children to stand near the card which describes how they feel about that activity or item. They do not have to stand on either Like or Not Like, they can stand in the space in between to indicate how much they like or dislike the activity / item.

You may find to begin with that they will stand with their friends. However, it is usual that after a couple of attempts they will choose to be more independent – being different starts to become fun. You can extend this activity by asking children to articulate why they are in their chosen place on the continuum. This is also a lovely opportunity for children to discover new things about their friends, family or classmates – who likes what and why and who doesn't like what and why.

- Swimming
- Going on a roller coaster
- Speaking in assembly
- The colour blue
- Break time at school
- Pepperoni pizza
- Singing
- Dancing
- Football

Please add your own ideas to the list

(If a child does choose to stand with their friend, gently challenge and encourage them to own their difference.)

- *Is it ok to like different things to your friends?*
- *Why might some people think they have to like what their friends like?*
- *Can it be more interesting to like different things? Perhaps you can then introduce your friends to something new.*

Are there any children in the class who do activities that are unusual or different?

If so encourage them to share with the class.

We all like to fit in with friends so it can feel awkward to be different. But if they don't care about difference then it shows that friendship is more important than being different.

Activity – More Superpowers

You can use **Appendix 1** again here if you wish.

If kindness is a superpower how about these?

- Difference
- Friendship
- Language

Discuss what is powerful about each of them.

Discussion starters

Difference

- *What is powerful about being different?*
- *What is powerful about accepting difference?*
- *What can we learn from differences?*

Friendship

- *What is powerful about friendship?*
- *What does it mean to be a friend?*
- *How do you behave towards your friends?*
- *What do you do for your friends?*

Encourage children to see how important and meaningful friendship can be.

Language

- *Language is a very powerful instrument.*
- *The words we choose to say can be helpful or harmful.*
- *We can speak words of encouragement, praise, inspiration and enthusiasm.*
- *We can also speak words of threat, hatefulness, put downs and criticism.*
- *And once unkind words have been said they are hard to take back. They can sometimes leave a mess that is very hard to clean up – imagine that words are like eggs. We have to treat them carefully – if we don't they can leave a horrible mess.*
- *We also have to own the words that we say – they belong to us, no-one else. If we make a bad joke or say an unkind thing, we cannot then blame the other person for not getting the joke or being upset. They are **our** words and we have to take responsibility for them.*

The language of kindness is:

- *Positive and supportive*
- *Clear, so it isn't misunderstood*
- *Inclusive, so no-one is left out*
- *Belongs to us – what I say are my words, I choose to say them so they are my responsibility. I cannot blame anyone else for the words I choose to say.*

The children can now choose either friendship, difference or language and design a new superhero, describing how their new superhero would use their superpower.

These new superpowers are all elements of kindness.

So kindness isn't about agreeing with or liking someone else but about accepting them and upholding their right to feel safe. It is about an absence of cruelty, meanness and nastiness.

If we do get it wrong it is important to forgive ourselves and commit to doing better and getting it right next time. Just like anything else, the more we practise, the better we get.

The right to feel safe and the language of safety are both elements of Protective Behaviours, explored and endorsed by the work of The Protective Behaviours Consortium and the Feeling Safe Foundation.

How did Ling use her superpower?

The learning here is that Ling was able to go against what her dance class friends were saying and doing.

- She listened to Danny's new ideas even though they may have been very different to hers.
- Ling supported Danny's ideas and they worked together to create a different dance.
- The bonus was that the judges really liked that Ling and Danny were different from everyone else.

So KINDNESS can be

- *Celebrating how different we all are*
- *The best way to make friends*
- *Really easy!*

What else can KINDNESS be?

Session 6
Cool to be Kind

This is now the opportunity for the children to reflect on everything they have discussed and thought about whilst working through the book and the activities.

Read pages 17–20 in the book *Cool to be Kind*.

Activity – Kindness Cards

You will need a set of cards from *Appendix 9 – 'Cool to be Kind Cards'*. These can be used in a variety of ways:

- for you to give to children
- for children to give to others
- for children to give to themselves
- to thank anyone for being brilliant (in any way), being kind, helping, looking out for someone else, smiling
- as starter ideas for children to design their own **'Cool to be Kind Cards'**

To continue the theme of kindness there are a number of activities that can become part of a school week, or a regular way to start a session if working with an individual child.

Activity – Kindness Reflection

Introduce a 'kindness reflection'. In schools this could be done on a Monday morning and Friday afternoon.

On Monday morning

Head on table, eyes closed (if the child/children feel comfortable doing this).
Spend 1 minute thinking about:

- The kind people you know
- Kind acts that someone has done for you

- *A kind act that you could do for someone*
- *What does kindness mean to you?*
- *How do you show kindness?*
- *What more can you do to be kind or show kindness?*
- *What can you do today or this week that is kind?*

And on Friday

- *What have you done this week that is kind?*
- *What can you do this weekend that is kind?*

Activity – Kindness Presentation

Just as Coco, Otto, Ollie and Ling do in the book, ask the children to work in small groups, or individually, to explore and create a presentation on kindness.

You might wish to allocate areas of research – charities, being a playground buddy, random acts of kindness, the kindness that was seen during the corona virus lockdown, poems about kindness, songs about kindness – or allow the children to choose what kindness means to them.

They can share kind deeds that they have done and suggest things that their group, class, school, club, family can do.

Kindness in the classroom / at home / in the community

The choice to be kind – reminders and reinforcers that can be seen and heard on a daily basis. Displays of pictures, poems, statements, images of the characters from the book, language of kindness being used.

Random acts of kindness – lots of examples to be found on the internet; little acts don't have to cost any money, a smile, a helping hand, a kind word, a kind message, a homemade card (see Session 3 activity 'Three Acts of Kindness').

Charities – investigate what charities do, who they are, when they started, how money is raised, who they help.

Friendship benches – children can be taught skills to support other children who may be struggling to make friends. In a school playground a designated area can be identified where children can just sit and chat.

Peer mentors – children can be taught skills to support other children in the classroom, paired readers, buddy working.

Playground Buddies – similar to Friendship benches, children can be on alert in the playground to invite others to join in games, to read or to chat.

Secret spy – choose a 'helper' to report back to you whenever they see another child being kind. At the end of the day / week tell the group / class who has been seen being kind to others.

Lucky dip – if it is feasible, make available a box or bag from which those children who have been chosen by others for their kindness can 'dip' for a small gift (sweets, pens, mini collectables/toys, etc).

Affirmations – see Cool to be Kind Cards.

I saw this and thought of you – kindness quotes that can be presented by you or the children.

Award cards – for things such as biggest smile, best joke teller, most helpful.

Please reinforce that Coco and her friends chose to be kind even when others were choosing to be unkind. This can be very hard to do sometimes which is why it is important to be strong like a superhero. It is much easier to follow what everyone else is doing, which is why being different can be a superpower too.

Help children to become deliberate in their actions – to notice what they are doing and saying, and make a conscious choice to be kind. To use their energy wisely, like a superpower.

A few extra ideas

Discussion Disrupters

Here are some extra questions to use in the discussions if you find the children are not as forthcoming as you would like.

- *Is there anything in that part of the book you would like to talk about?*
- *What did you think of.....................?*
- *Why do you think that?*
- *Who agrees / disagrees? Why?*
- *Do you think that was fair? Right? OK? Acceptable?*
- *Do you think that was unfair? Wrong? Unacceptable?*
- *What might have happened if....?*
- *Who do you feel most sorry for? Why?*
- *What would you have done?*
- *If that happened to someone here how could we help put it right?*
- *What's an unkind thing you've done and how did you put it right? How can you put it right?*

World Kindness Day

Celebrate World Kindness Day every November 13th and National Random Acts of Kindness Day every February 17th.

Create a classroom / clubroom / family Kindness Calendar

For example:

- Make someone smile Monday
- Tell a joke Tuesday
- Welcoming Wednesday
- Think of others Thursday
- Friendly Friday

(probably impossible to always be alliterative!)

Explore literature that shows unkindness and kindness

- *Wonder* – RJ Palacio
- *Jane Eyre* – Charlotte Brontë
- *Charlie and the Chocolate Factory* – Roald Dahl
- *Cliffhanger* – Jacqueline Wilson

- *The Boy in the Striped Pyjamas* – John Boyne
- *Matilda* – Roald Dahl
- *The Lion, the Witch and the Wardrobe* – CS Lewis
- *The Jungle Book* – Rudyard Kipling
- *The BFG* – Roald Dahl
- *The Boy in the Dress* – David Walliams
- *Sleepovers* – Jacqueline Wilson

... for starters

So KINDNESS can be

- *Everywhere*

And KINDNESS can be

- *Cool!*

Self-kindness

An extra or stand-alone session

"There are more things … likely to frighten us than there are to crush us; we suffer more often in imagination than in reality."

Seneca, Roman Philosopher

This session can be included as part of the whole delivery. It also stands alone to support specific children who may be struggling with self-esteem.

There are some children whose unkind narrative is a repetition of what has been said to them by others – both adults and children. A child who is unkind to others may be repeating the unkindnesses done to them. And may be reinforcing those unkindnesses to themselves. Please be aware of the safeguarding procedures in your setting.

Self-kindness needs to be cultivated, looked after and practised. It is about being sensitive to our own feelings as well as the feelings of others, particularly negative feelings and negative thoughts.

Some children can be self-critical to the extent that it prevents them from developing, moving forward and achieving. This self-criticism may be heard by others but it is often hidden in the head of the child. Their anger, frustration and disappointment are reinforced by their internal voice, thus maintaining the negative emotions and potentially making them worse. So this session will include challenging negative self-talk, not believing their thoughts and accepting themselves

I can think to myself 'I am a green elephant' but that does not make it real. Thinking I am a green elephant does not make me a green elephant.

Someone can say to me 'You are a purple pumpkin'. I can choose to agree and live as though I am a purple pumpkin. Am I happy to think of myself that way? Does it help me? If not, I can choose to disagree. I am not, never have been and never will be a purple pumpkin. And someone saying I am still does not make me a purple pumpkin.

Activity – I'm a Purple Pumpkin

Say 'I'm a purple pumpkin' 20 times to yourself.

Are you a purple pumpkin?

Probably not!

The things we say to ourselves doesn't always make them true.

We can say true things – 'I am 9 years old', 'I am a boy', 'I am a 12-year-old girl'.

It is important to know which things we say help us, are kind, help us to feel good and which things are mean and unkind and things we wouldn't say to our best friend. And to know that we can choose which we say.

Activity – Mean Mate / Patient Pal

Imagine you are playing a game with two friends when you make a mistake, or you get something wrong. Your two friends react differently.

Mean Mate is quick to criticise you, points out what you got wrong and blames you, they tell others about your mistake, they are impatient, unkind and tell you off.

On a piece of paper divided in half write down some of the things that Mean Mate might say.

Patient Pal knows your mistake wasn't deliberate, Patient Pal is calm and supportive, encourages you, looks forward and is forgiving.

Now write down some of the things that Patient Pal might say.

For example:

Mean Mate	Patient Pal
You're stupid	It's ok
You always get stuff wrong	You can do it
What's wrong with you?	Shall we have another go?
You're no good at anything	Let's ask for help

Who would you want to spend more time with? Who would you turn to if you had a problem? Who would you ask for help?

We all have both Mean Mate and Patient Pal inside us. Sometimes one pops up more than the other. If it is Mean Mate then we can feel worthless, a failure, stupid, like there is something wrong with us. But if it is Patient Pal who pops up, then we are helping ourselves to feel ok and to feel stronger.

We can choose who to invite into our heads, Mean Mate or Patient Pal. Why choose Mean Mate when we can choose Patient Pal?

Activity – My Map of Me

You can revisit this activity from Session 3 to remind the children that there are lots of versions of us, that we are all made up of different parts – some great, some not so great.

- Create a Map of Me using Mean Mate parts and Patient Pal parts.
- Create a 'best version of me' Map.
- What are the parts I really want?
- What can I do to get there?
- Who can help me get there?

We sometimes have to put up with getting things wrong or feeling different, being sad or angry. We all experience these things and these feelings aren't wrong. Getting something wrong doesn't make you wrong about everything. Getting something wrong usually means that next time you'll get it right because you have learnt something.

(There are lots of examples on the internet of successful people who made mistakes and got things wrong in the early part of their careers.

- *The first Harry Potter book by J.K. Rowling was rejected by 12 publishers before being accepted.*
- *The KFC recipe was rejected by over a 1000 people!*
- *"I have failed over and over again in my life. And that is why I succeed." Michael Jordan)*

Activity – My Kind Cards

You will need a copy of *Appendix 10 – 'Kind to Me Cards'* for each child.

Go through the cards and talk about what they mean:

- **Well done me** – *use positive self-talk as often as possible*
- **Stand like a tree** – *look at how tree trunks are wider at the bottom, this gives them stability. Try standing with feet apart to 'plant' yourself firmly*
- **Don't get cross at myself for getting cross at myself** – *if you get cross at yourself, notice it and know you can stop it*
- **I won't always feel like this** – *feelings are like the weather, they come and they go*
- **Visualise Mean Mate shrinking into the distance** – *imagine a picture of Mean Mate and make them smaller and smaller until they disappear*
- **Visualise Patient Pal growing bigger and bigger** – *imagine a picture of Patient Pal and make them as big or bigger than you*
- **It's ok I thought that but next time I can choose a kinder thought** – *notice it, don't tell yourself off, choose kindness next time*
- **I can ask for help** – *a friend or a trusted adult*
- **I can do this** – *yes you can, have a go, you never know*
- **I don't have to be perfect – no-one else is** – *absolutely no-one, at all, anywhere!*
- **It's ok to get something wrong – it doesn't mean I am wrong** – *there is no law or rule about getting things wrong or making mistakes and everyone does it sometimes*
- **Am I a purple pumpkin?** – *choose the best, kindest words to say to yourself*

Children can choose the cards that they like the best or they can make their own.

Cut into single cards, decorate them, and keep them in a tin, in a box, in a pocket, in a tray, turn into bookmarks… and look at them whenever needed.

Remind children that positive self-talk is not just *what* we say to ourselves but *how* we say it.

If a child finds it difficult to think about saying nice things to themselves, continue with the idea that it is Patient Pal talking to them – they may be able to tolerate this better.

There are more suggestions of positive self-talk in the *Myg and Me* book.

Some final thoughts

We are always going to meet people who are stronger, cleverer, taller – being kind to ourselves means that we do not have to decide who is 'best' or who is 'worst', it means that we can allow ourselves to be different.

- If we 'feed' Mean Mate – the part of us that is critical, envious, inferior and angry – then these will be our strengths.
- If we 'feed' Patient Pal – the part of us that is joyous, kind, forgiving and compassionate – these will be our strengths.

Being kind to yourself is not being weak or selfish.

Being kind to yourself is strong, is deserved and is inside you.

It's OK if you don't change overnight. There is no need to tell yourself that you 'must' or 'have to' or 'should', you can do this at your own speed if you are willing. Be open, listen to your thoughts and challenge them if they are not helping you. If you have ever changed your mind about anything – your favourite colour, your favourite band, your favourite pizza topping – then you can change your mind about what you say to yourself. And that is so much more important than what you put on your pizza! Imagine finding a diamond so rare that there isn't another one like it in the whole world. How would you look after that diamond? Would you treat it gently and carefully? Would you look after it? Would you protect it and cherish it?

I think you would... and guess what?

You are that diamond.

And remember, there is **always** a choice. We can choose to be kind to others and we can choose to be kind to ourselves.

> *So what else can KINDNESS be?*
>
> *... It means I can be kind to me.*

Appendix 1
Superpowers

Appendix 2
Feelings

How might Kez have been feeling when the goals went past him?

How might Kez have been feeling when the team lost the match?

How might Kez have been feeling when he heard his team mates talking?

How might Kez have been feeling when he volunteered?

Copyright material from Liz Slamer (2021), *A Practical Resource for Negotiating the World of Friendships and Relationships*, Routledge

Appendix 3
How Might it Feel?

Appendix 4
Calm

BREATHING	RELAXING
VISUALISING	SHARING

BREATHING	RELAXING
VISUALISING	SHARING

Appendix 5
My Map of Me

Lazy me – I didn't take my dirty plate into the kitchen	**Smiley me** – I smiled at my teacher when I arrived at school
Nervous me – I didn't speak to my mum's friend	**Funny me** – I tell the best jokes
Impatient me – I shouted at my brother because he took ages to get his shoes on	**Calm me** – I calmed my friend when she was nervous
Forgetful me – I forgot to take my dad's birthday card home to give him	**Kind me** – I made my mum's friend a thank you card for looking after me
Mean me – I didn't tell my friend I had some sweets so that I didn't have to share them	**Friendly me** – I invited a new classmate to my party

Appendix 6
Thoughts

What might Nina be thinking?
Write Nina's thoughts inside her head. You will need three colours.

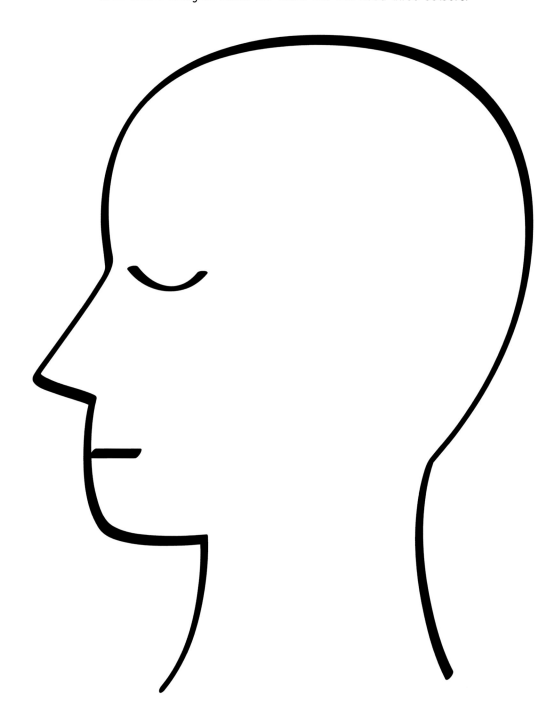

Appendix 7
Send a 'Cool to be Kind' Message

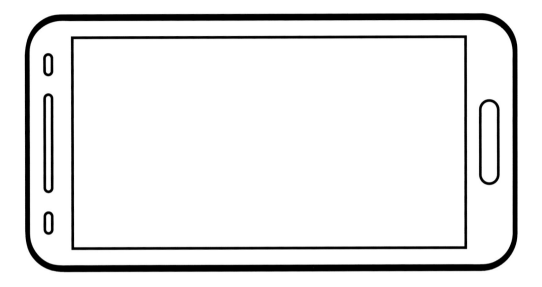

Appendix 8
Like / Not Like Continuum Cards

LIKE

NOT LIKE

Appendix 9
Cool to be Kind Cards

This week I will … Monday Tuesday Wednesday Thursday Friday	This weekend I will … Saturday Sunday
You are amazing because … YOU	I am amazing because … ME
Thank you for … THANK YOU	See you on Monday, let's …
I was cool to be kind when …	I challenged my Mean Mate mind when I …
I increased 'My Map of Me' *best parts* when …	I decreased 'My Map of Me' *not so good parts* when ….

Appendix 10
Kind to Me Cards

WELL DONE ME	IT'S OK I THOUGHT THAT BUT NEXT TIME I CAN CHOOSE A KINDER THOUGHT
STAND LIKE A TREE	I CAN ASK FOR HELP
DON'T GET CROSS AT MYSELF FOR GETTING CROSS AT MYSELF	I CAN DO THIS
I WON'T ALWAYS FEEL LIKE THIS	I DON'T HAVE TO BE PERFECT NO-ONE ELSE IS
VISUALISE MEAN MATE SHRINKING INTO THE DISTANCE	IT'S OK TO GET SOMETHING WRONG IT DOESN'T MEAN I AM WRONG
VISUALISE PATIENT PAL GROWING BIGGER AND BIGGER	AM I A PURPLE PUMPKIN?